MARTIAL ARTS IN ACTION

# JUDO AND JUJITSU

MARTIAL ARTS IN ACTION

# JUDO AND JUJITSU

BY CAROL ELLIS

mc Marshall Cavendish
Benchmark
New York

Published by Marshall Cavendish Benchmark
An imprint of Marshall Cavendish Corporation

Other Marshall Cavendish Offices:
Marshall Cavendish International (Asia) Private Limited, 1 New Industrial Road, Singapore
536196 • Marshall Cavendish International (Thailand) Co Ltd. 253 Asoke, 12th Flr, Sukhumvit
21 Road, Klongtoey Nua, Wattana, Bangkok 10110, Thailand • Marshall Cavendish (Malaysia)
Sdn Bhd, Times Subang, Lot 46, Subang Hi-Tech Industrial Park, Batu Tiga,
40000 Shah Alam, Selangor Darul Ehsan, Malaysia

Marshall Cavendish is a trademark of Times Publishing Limited

Library of Congress Cataloging-in-Publication Data

Ellis, Carol, 1945-
Judo and jujitsu / Carol Ellis.
p. cm. — (Martial arts in action)
Includes index.
ISBN 978-0-7614-4933-1 (print)
ISBN 978-1-60870-363-0 (ebook)
1. Judo—Juvenile literature. 2. Jiu-jitsu—Juvenile literature. I. Title.
GV1114.E55 2012
796.815'2—dc22
2010013821

Editor: Peter Mavrikis
Publisher: Michelle Bisson
Art Director: Anahid Hamparian
Series design by Kristen Branch

Photo Research by Candlepants Incorporated

Cover Photo: Tom & DeeAnn McCarthy/Corbis

The photographs in this book are used by permission and through the courtesy of:
Corbis: © Dimitri Iundt/TempSport,2; Duomo. 9. Alamy Images: imagebroker, 6; Forget Patrick/
SagaPhoto.com, 8; Claude Thibault, 22, 40; Eye Ubiquitous, 26; Amana Photos Inc., 30; Adrian
Sherratt, 31; Photo Japan, 42. Getty Images: Tony Hopewell, 10, 27; DEA/Dagli Orti, 13; Hulton
Archive, 17; Jamie McDonald, 20; Andy Crawford, 24; Stefano Oppo, 29; Amwell, 35; Andreanna
Seymore, 36; Steve Shott, 38; Bob Elsdale, 43. The Image Works: Roger Viollet, 16. The Bridgeman
Art Library: Private Collection Archives Charmin, 21. Shutterstock: M.E. Mulder, 33.

Printed in Malaysia (T)
1 3 5 6 4 2

# CONTENTS

CHAPTER ONE
## JUDO CLASS 7

CHAPTER TWO
## THE HISTORY OF JUDO AND JUJITSU 13

CHAPTER THREE
## GETTING STARTED 25

CHAPTER FOUR
## JUDO, JUJITSU, AND YOU 39

GLOSSARY 44
FIND OUT MORE 46
INDEX 47

**CHAPTER ONE**

# JUDO CLASS

WHEN DAVID WAS ELEVEN, he and his best friend signed up for judo classes. David did not know much about martial arts except what he had seen in movies or video games, in which a character defeated the bad guys with just a few flying kicks. He knew the real thing would not be like that. But he also knew that he was not the most athletic person in the world. He had played soccer, and he liked shooting hoops, but he was not very good at either of them. In fact, he was pretty clumsy. But he wanted to give judo a try.

David, his friend, and his parents went to the community center and watched a class of kids about his own age practice judo. The students attempted to throw each other to the mat and tried to **pin**

*PEOPLE CAN BEGIN STUDYING THE MARTIAL ARTS AT ALMOST ANY AGE.*

each other down. It was pretty impressive seeing a scrawny kid sweep a heavier one's leg out from under him, then throw him flat on his back. David was right—it was very different from movies and video games. But even though it did not look easy, it looked like fun. A week later, David and his friend joined the judo class.

A year later, they are both almost ready to move up in rank, from a yellow belt to a green belt. Like all beginners, David started with a white belt, and the first thing he learned was how to fall without getting hurt. It was a good thing he did, because during practice, he got thrown as often as he threw! And knowing how to fall turned

JUDO AND JUJITSU STUDENTS NEED TO LEARN MANY SKILLS, INCLUDING THROWING, GRAPPLING, AND PINNING TECHNIQUES.

PADDED MATTING HELPS TO KEEP MARTIAL ARTISTS
SAFE DURING TRAINING AND COMPETITION.

out to come in handy when he slipped on an icy sidewalk or tripped over the dog in the middle of the night.

Learning different ways to fall, throw, or pin someone to the mat took a lot of practice, and a lot of concentration. In judo, you had to **focus** hard and pay attention if you wanted to get any better. It was like what his teachers were always saying in school. And when he thought about it, he realized that ever since he started taking judo, he did not have as much trouble paying attention in school as he used to. Although he was not acing every test, he was doing better. His parents thought it was because of judo, and maybe they were right. He was sure of one thing: since he had started judo, he could run farther and faster than ever. And when playing basketball with friends, he was much more coordinated and faster on his feet.

One of the things he liked best about judo was working with a partner. They gave each other tips and tried to figure out what they were doing wrong so they could both get better at it.

Before judo, David was not thrilled about competing because he was afraid he would mess up. But he had been to some local judo tournaments, and even though he did not win, at least he had not been afraid to try. He knew he was pretty good, and he knew he could be even better if he just kept working at it.

# THE HISTORY OF JUDO AND JUJITSU

CHAPTER TWO

**J**UDO IS A MARTIAL ART that grew out of an ancient Japanese fighting system called **jujitsu**. In the early history of Japan, powerful families known as **clans** battled for years over control of the land. The clans hired warriors to protect and defend them. These professional warriors were called **samurai**. Skilled in combat, groups of armored samurai would clash in deadly battles. The samurai were experts at fighting from horseback, using spears and razor-sharp swords to kill their enemies.

But what happened when a samurai lost his sword during battle and found himself facing an enemy on the ground? For this kind of hand-to-hand combat, the samurai developed **techniques** that

*A HEAVILY ARMED SAMURAI WARRIOR.*

JAPANESE CHILDREN HAVE STUDIED JUJITSU FOR CENTURIES.

became known as jujitsu. Jujitsu taught the samurai ways to throw, kick, punch, and strangle a rival who was stronger or still armed. Even if a samurai did have a weapon, knowledge of jujitsu could make him much more likely to succeed.

Over time, hundreds of jujitsu schools developed. Some taught the use of weapons and some did not. Some focused on throwing techniques and others on striking and kicking. Even in training, jujitsu could be brutal, with painful nerve strikes, leg and arm twists, and lethal kicks.

# THE BEGINNING OF JUDO

By the middle of the 1800s, the days of the dueling samurai were over in Japan. A lot of people stopped doing jujitsu, because it was now being used by gangs of criminals and in exhibitions just to make money. Still, many schools remained and taught their art of hand-to-hand combat. It was in one of these schools that a young man from Tokyo first learned jujitsu.

Jigoro Kano was the youngest of three sons. As a child, he was small, weak, and a frequent target of bullies. He was determined to grow stronger and learn how to defend himself, and jujitsu seemed the perfect way to do that. Kano studied at several jujitsu schools and became a master in the art. At one of the schools, he kept getting defeated by an opponent who outweighed him by 100 pounds (45 kilograms). This frustrated him so much that he began to develop his own techniques. Eventually, he defeated that heavier opponent.

JIGORO KANO, CREATOR OF JUDO.

Using the techniques he had come up with, Kano formed his own style of martial art. By then, he was a school principal and the president of Japan's Physical Education Society. He wanted a martial art that could be taught in physical education classes. He got rid of the most dangerous techniques and changed others so they would be safe to practice. He called his new art judo.

Judo quickly became popular in Japan. People especially liked the way Kano taught students to respect each other. At the same time, jujitsu was making a comeback. The police were thinking of

EVEN AS AN ELDERLY MAN, JIGORO KANO REMAINED A HIGHLY SKILLED MARTIAL ARTIST.

teaching it as a way to restrain criminals. Many people admired judo, but could it really stand up to jujitsu as a way to fight or **subdue** someone? Rivalry grew between the two arts, and in 1886, the Tokyo Police held a grand competition between Kano's judo school and the most famous jujitsu school. In that tournament, the judo fighters won all but two of the matches, and those two ended in a tie. Judo

U.S. SOLDIERS PRACTICING JUDO IN THE 1950S.

# What Do Jujitsu and Judo Mean?

In Japanese, jujitsu means "gentle art." Gentle might seem a strange word for a fighting technique, but in the world of martial arts, gentle means the use of skill to outdo a physically stronger opponent. Jujitsu was developed so that a samurai warrior could defeat a rival who might be heavily armed and protected by body armor.

Judo combines the word "ju," with the word "do," which means "way." So judo means "gentle way." Jigoro Kano chose this name because he believed that judo was not only a martial art, it was also a way of educating the mind and the spirit. He wanted judo to be useful in all parts of a student's life.

became part of the Japanese physical education system, and it was taught to the police. During World War II, a group of U.S. soldiers called the American Judo Club taught judo to other troops. Judo was on its way, and began to spread around the world.

Jujitsu did not die out just because judo became popular. The American military taught jujitsu to soldiers early in the twentieth century, and it is still used by police, the military, and security forces.

## JUDO AND JUJITSU TODAY

Today, people of all ages study judo and jujitsu. Some study them for exercise because they give the muscles and heart such a great workout. Some people learn them as a way of self-defense. While both arts are still used by police and the military, they are also widely practiced as sports. Judo became an Olympic sport in 1964. One style of sport jujitsu is practiced in the World Games.

Most jujitsu schools have changed the art so it is not dangerous to practice. But just as in the days of the samurai, jujitsu has many styles. There are two main types of sport jujitsu: a **self-defense** demonstration, in which the attacker and the defender come from the same team and demonstrate defense techniques, and a fighting system, where competitors use striking and grappling as a means of defeating an opponent. Some jujitsu styles are like traditional Japanese jujitsu and some are more modern. One of the most popular forms is Brazilian jujitsu (BJJ). An expert student of Jigoro Kano's named Mitsuyo Maeda moved to Brazil and opened his first judo academy around 1921. There, he taught judo and jujitsu to a young man named Carlos Gracie. Over the years, the Gracie family developed

TOURNAMENT COMPETITION HELPS EVEN THE MOST ADVANCED MARTIAL ARTISTS SHARPEN THEIR SKILLS.

the Brazilian style of jujitsu. BJJ uses throws, but it is most famous for its groundwork, the methods used to defeat an opponent once he or she is on the mat. Japanese jujitsu places importance on standing techniques, while Brazilian jujitsu focuses more on what happens on

# FAMOUS PEOPLE WHO HAVE USED JUDO AND JUJITSU

United States President Theodore Roosevelt began to train in judo while he was in office. He even set aside a room in the White House for judo practice. He eventually earned a brown belt.

British author Sir Arthur Conan Doyle had his master detective, Sherlock Holmes, use jujitsu to defeat his enemy in one of his famous stories. Vladimir Putin, the Prime Minister of Russia, is a black belt in judo. He co-wrote a book on the subject, and in 2008, he even put out a judo instructional DVD.

A FRENCH MAGAZINE ILLUSTRATION SHOWS A JUJITSU CLASS IN 1903.

**WARMING UP BEFORE A COMPETITION.**

the mat. Other martial arts such as Russian sambo, Korean hapkido, and western-style wrestling use jujitsu-like techniques.

Once judo and jujitsu became popular competitive martial arts, clubs and classes started to teach them. Organizations like the International Jujitsu Federation and the International Judo Federation sponsor training camps and tournaments. One important judo group is the Kodokan Institute, the original school of judo founded by Jigoro Kano in 1882. The Kodokan offers classes to anyone who wants to study judo. Students who are truly devoted to judo rent rooms and live there while they continue their training.

# CHAPTER THREE

# GETTING STARTED

**I**F YOU DECIDE TO STUDY JUDO OR JUJITSU, you need to find a *dojo*, a training or practice hall where you can take classes. This might not have been very easy fifty years ago. But today, kids and adults by the millions study martial arts. Maybe someone you know is already studying one of the arts and can recommend a place. A look in the yellow pages under "martial" arts or an Internet search will show you the clubs, community centers, and even colleges in your area that offer classes.

Most dojos welcome visitors, and many of them offer free classes to let you get a feel for what training will be like. So it is a good idea to check out a few dojos to make sure it is the right place for you.

*TWO MARTIAL ARTISTS FACE EACH OTHER ON THE DOJO FLOOR.*

JUDO STUDENTS TRAINING UNDER THEIR SENSEI'S WATCHFUL EYE.

Are there plenty of students about your age, and are they enjoying the class? What is the **sensei**, or teacher, like? Does he or she take time to explain things, especially to the beginners? Some people like competition and some do not. Does a dojo require you to compete to move up in rank?

## CLOTHING

In some dojos, you can take the first couple of classes wearing sweatpants and a T-shirt, but after that you will need a martial arts

# ETIQUETTE

"Before and after practicing judo or engaging in a match, opponents bow to each other. Bowing is an expression of gratitude and respect. In effect, you are thanking your opponent for giving you the opportunity to improve your technique." Jigoro Kano, founder of judo.

The *rei*, or bow, is part of the judo tradition, and most jujitsu classes use it, too. In most dojos, students bow to the sensei, to their training partners, and at the beginning and end of class.

BY BOWING BEFORE A MATCH, THESE YOUNG GIRLS DISPLAY RESPECT FOR EACH OTHER AND FOR THE MARTIAL ART THEY PRACTICE.

uniform called a *gi*. Judo gis and jujitsu gis consist of loose-fitting drawstring pants, a jacket, and a belt. Because the gis have to stand up to a lot of grabbing, twisting, and pulling, they are made of strong cotton, with extra material in the collar, lapels, and armpits.

A gi has no zippers, buttons, or pockets. Students do not wear any jewelry while practicing. All of these things could scratch the fighters or get snagged on something and cause injuries. Judo and jujitsu are practiced barefoot.

## TECHNIQUES AND TRAINING

One of the main ideas behind both judo and jujitsu is that you do not need pure strength to overcome an opponent. With the right mix of balance, leverage, and timing, you can use your opponent's strength and momentum against him.

Instead of using force against force, both arts teach the technique of "giving way." Jigoro Kano gave an example of this: "Suppose that my opponent leans forward and pushes me with one hand. This puts him off balance. If I grab him by the upper sleeve of his outstretched arm, pivot so that my back is close to his chest, clamp my free hand on his shoulder and suddenly bend over, he will go flying over my head and land flat on his back."

Judo and jujitsu are designed for close, hand-to-hand combat and use many of the same techniques. Knowing how to fall without getting hurt is a crucial part of both arts. One of the first things you learn are the different types of **breakfalls**: backwards, to the side, to the front, and a shoulder, or rolling fall. If you watch someone

A BLACK BELT IS EVIDENCE OF MANY YEARS OF HARD WORK.

getting thrown in a match, you may hear a loud "bang," as they hit the mat. It sounds painful, but it is really a technique. Slapping their arms against the mat helps break the fall.

Judo may be famous for its spectacular throws, but once you have an opponent on the mat, you need to know how to keep him there until he submits. To do this, you learn groundwork such as **holds**, armlocks, and chokes.

MARTIAL ARTS COMPETITION REQUIRES BOTH PHYSICAL SKILL AND MENTAL DISCIPLINE.

IT IS VERY IMPORTANT TO WARM UP AND
STRETCH BEFORE PRACTICE.

Jujitsu began as a form of mortal combat, but today it is an art of self-defense and a sport. It teaches you to flow from one technique to another so you can control your opponent. Jujitsu has many styles, and usually teaches defensive moves such as wrist grabs and bear hugs. Like judo, it uses throws, armlocks, and chokes. Unlike judo, some styles of jujitsu use open hand, fist and elbow strikes, low kicks and knee strikes, and joint locks.

Judo and jujitsu classes always begin with warm-up exercises to build your **stamina** and keep your muscles flexible. Some are the kinds of exercises you might have in gym class, like push-ups and sit-ups, leg stretches, and jumping jacks. Others are turned into games, such as crab crawl races and jumping from side to side over a belt held by two partners.

After warming up, the sensei will teach a new technique, then students will partner up and practice it together, along with the moves that were already learned. Helping your partner learn and do his or her best is an important part of training.

Another part of training is **randori**, or free practice. You work with a partner again, but this time, neither of you knows which move the other is going to make. Randori gives you both the chance to test your skills as if you were in a match.

**Kata** is another style of training. The word *kata* means "forms." Partners perform a series of movements that demonstrate their skills in different techniques.

When you first start learning judo or jujitsu, you will wear a white belt. Belt colors show your level of achievement, or rank. There are two divisions: students, or **kyus**, and masters, or **dans**. Students

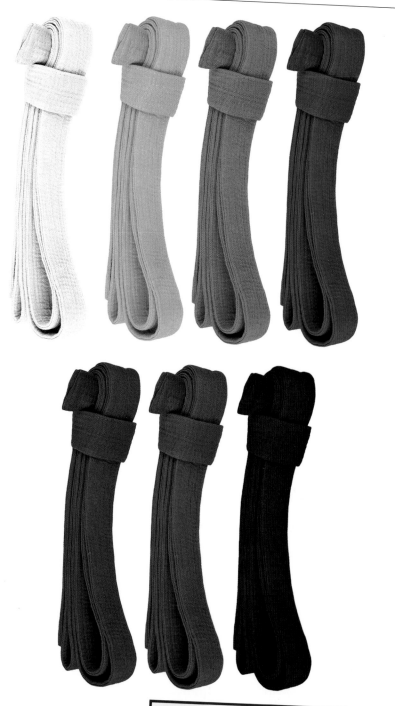

THE BELT SYSTEM IS USED IN JUDO, JUJITSU, AND MANY OTHER MARTIAL ARTS TO SHOW THE LEVEL OF SKILL A STUDENT HAS ATTAINED.

start with white belts and progress through colored ones, usually yellow, orange, green, blue, purple, and brown.

There are ten dan levels. In jujitsu, all dans wear black belts. In judo, dans start with black, but the highest ranking dans wear red belts. A student usually has to be older than seventeen to earn a brown or black belt. Most dojos have a set list of techniques for each belt color. To get promoted, students need to show they have learned these techniques.

## BASIC ELEMENTS IN JUDO

- Throws are done by unbalancing opponents, then using leverage to throw them. Types of throws include hip, shoulder, and neck throws.
- Holds are used to keep an opponent on the mat. Types of holds include the scarf hold (in which one arm becomes a "scarf" around the opponent's neck), shoulder holds, and chest holds.
- Armlocks are used to restrain an opponent by applying pressure to his or her elbow joint. Players use their legs, stomach, knees, and armpits to gain an armlock.
- Chokes, or strangleholds, are accomplished by gripping an opponent around the neck and upper body.

## BASIC JUJITSU MOVES

Basic elements in jujitsu are the same as in judo. Some styles include kicks, strikes, and joint locks. Moves that could be dangerous are not taught to younger students.

THIS PHOTOGRAPH CAPTURES THE SPEED AND INTENSITY OF JUDO COMPETITION.

- Kicks and strikes are blows to the body with a fist, arm, elbow, leg, knee, or foot. Jujitsu fighters use them to distract or unbalance an opponent.
- Joint locks pressure a joint such as the wrist, elbow, shoulder, or ankle in a way it is not supposed to bend.

## COMPETITION

Competing in tournaments is another way to test your ability in judo or jujitsu. Tournaments are held at the local, state, and national levels

A BLACK BELT IN JUJITSU PINS HIS OPPONENT TO THE MAT.

and reach as high as the Olympics for judo, and the World Games for sport jujitsu. Contestants are divided into weight categories, so everyone competes against people their own size.

In a judo match, the goal is to score an *ippon*, or one full point.

Once that is done, the match is over. You can score an ippon by throwing your opponent flat on his or her back, or by holding your opponent to the mat for twenty-five seconds. If this does not happen and time runs out, judges award half and quarter points for each contestant, then add them up. The contestant with the most points wins.

A match in sports jujitsu consists of three rounds. Judges award points for different techniques such as strikes and throws. The contestant with the most points at the end wins the match. Competitions are also held in kata. Judges award points not just for technique, but things like attitude, balance, harmony, and concentration.

# CHAPTER FOUR

# JUDO, JUJITSU, AND YOU

**W**HEN I FIRST STARTED JUJITSU, I wasn't sure if I was going to like it," said an eleven year-old girl from Texas. "After a few classes I saw how fun it was. It's great for anybody who's looking to get into a sport. I like it because everybody helps everybody. It can help build up your **self-esteem** by knowing you can stand up to bullies. It gives you a chance to go to different places and you get to meet people from everywhere."

Millions of people around the world study judo and jujitsu. Some start as young as six, while others do not begin until they are fifty, and the reasons they start are as different as their ages. Many people study them because they are fun activities, or because they need

*JUDO AND JUJITSU TECHNIQUES MAKE IT POSSIBLE TO DEFEAT EVEN A LARGER, STRONGER OPPONENT.*

A YOUNG JUDO STUDENT PROUDLY DISPLAYS
HIS ORANGE BELT.

the exercise. Some want to learn a method of self-defense or a sport they can compete in. No matter why you decide to study one of the arts, you will probably discover that you're learning much more than how to perform a throw or an armlock.

When you learn judo or jujitsu, you start out with a great advantage that you will not find in many other sports: you do not have to be taller or more muscular or able to run faster than anyone else. In both of the arts, you learn to use your opponent's strength against him or her. Knowing judo or jujitsu can give a small, slender person the **confidence** and ability to go up against a taller, stronger opponent.

Judo and jujitsu teach you to think on your feet so you do not wind up flat on your back. Your reflexes and coordination will definitely improve. If you practice other sports, you will find that studying judo or jujitsu will help your timing, your balance, and your ability to make split-second decisions. Improving your flexibility, balance, and coordination will help you not just in other sports, but in everyday situations such as icy sidewalks or unexpected falls. In judo and jujitsu, one of the first things you learn is how to fall without getting hurt!

Whether you practice one of the arts for fun or you want to compete, you will soon discover that judo and jujitsu have great health benefits. They strengthen your cardiovascular system—your heart and blood vessels. A good judo workout has been compared to lifting weights and running at the same time because it helps build muscles and also improves your lung capacity. And for anyone who is in danger of becoming a couch potato and wants to burn calories, judo and jujitsu will do the job!

# Paralympic Sport

Richard Favinger Jr. is a black belt in judo and a youth instructor at a Pennsylvania judo club. Scott Moore was a wrestler in high school. He started judo training in college and has competed internationally. Both men are legally blind.

Judo has been an official sport of the Paralympics since the middle of the 1980s. In fact, Scott Moore won the Gold Medal at the 2000 Sydney, Australia Paralympics.

Judo is a great sport for the blind or visually impaired. They can train or compete on equal ground with players who have full eyesight. This is because in many cases, you do not have to see your opponent; both of you are grappling with each other, so you know right where he or she is!

PHYSICAL DISABILITY DOES NOT HAVE TO KEEP ANYONE FROM STUDYING MARTIAL ARTS.

THE SKILL, DISCIPLINE, AND CONFIDENCE THESE YOUNG PEOPLE HAVE GAINED AT THE DOJO WILL STAY WITH THEM ALL THEIR LIVES.

Judo and jujitsu are not just good for your body, they are good for your mind. The concentration and focus you need to practice the arts may help you concentrate and focus better on your schoolwork. Respecting your opponent and helping others in your class will carry over into other situations in your life. When you study judo or jujitsu, you will learn to have more confidence in yourself. When you start, you will not know much about the sport. You will probably feel nervous. But if you keep working, pretty soon you will be tying a new colored belt around your waist. You may find that you are not nervous anymore. In fact, you are eager to reach the next level!

"By learning and mastering judo's essence from experience, we can always maintain composure, make decisions clearly, and foster self-esteem throughout our living in this complex society." Jigoro Kano, founder of judo.

# GLOSSARY

**breakfalls**—A way of breaking ones fall during practice or competition without suffering injury.

**clan**—A group of people sharing a common ancestry.

**confidence**—A feeling of certainty.

**dan**—A master of judo or jujitsu.

**dojo**—A school for the martial arts.

**etiquette**—A code of behavior.

**focus**—Strong concentration or attention on a certain subject or activity.

**gi**—A simple white robe worn by people who practice judo or some other Japanese martial art.

**holds**—A method of grasping or clutching one's opponent.

**jujitsu**—A Japanese martial art that uses no weapons and was developed for close combat.

**kata**—Forms or patterns of movements.

**kyu**—A judo or jujitsu student.

**pin**—To hold an opponent in place so that he or she cannot move.

**randori**—Free practice training.

**rei**—A formal bow performed to show respect.

**samurai**—A Japanese warrior.

**self-defense**—The act of defending oneself.

**self-esteem**—Having a sense of confidence or satisfaction in oneself.

**sensei**—A Japanese word for instructor or teacher.

**stamina**—Physical strength and endurance.

**subdue**—To defeat or bring under control.

**technique**—A special skill or set of movements.

FIND OUT MORE

BOOKS

Inman, Roy. *The Judo Handbook*. New York: Rosen Publishing, 2008.

Martin, Ashley. *How to Improve at Judo*. New York: Crabtree Publishing, 2009.

O'Shei, Tim. *Jujitsu*. Mankato, MN: Capstone Press, 2009.

Ribeirio, Saulo and Howell, Kevin. *Jiu-Jitsu University*. San Antonio, TX: Victory Belt Publishing, 2008.

WEBSITES

International Judo Federation
http://www.ijf.org

International Ju-Jitsu Federation
http://www.jjifweb.com/html/about.html

Kids Web Japan
http://web-japan.org/kidsweb/virtual/judo/index.html

United States Ju-Jitsu Federation
http://www.usjjf.org/info/into.htm

USA Judo
http://www.usjudo.org/index.asp

**INDEX**

Page numbers in **boldface** are illustrations.

American Judo Club, 19

belts, 32, **33,** 34
benefits of judo and jujitsu, 39, 41, 43
Brazilian Jujitsu (BJJ), 19–20, 23

clothing, 26, 28
competition, **20, 22, 35,** 35–37, **36**

etiquette, 27, **27**

falling, 28, 30
finding a school, 25–26

Gracie, Carlos, 19–20
groundwork, 30

health benefits, 39, 41, 43
history, 13–17, 19–20, 23

International Judo/Jujitsu Federations,
23

judo, basic elements, 34
judo, history, 15–17, 19
jujitsu, basic moves, 34–35
jujitsu, history, 13–14

Kano, Jigoro, **15,** 15–16, **16,** 18, 27,
28, 43
Kodokan Institute, 23

Maeda, Mitsuyo, 19–20
masters, 32, 34

military training, **17,** 19

Olympics, 19, 36

Paralympics, 42, **42**
police training, 16–17, 19
Putin, Vladimir, 21

respect, 27, **27**
Roosevelt, Theodore, 21

samurai warriors, **12,** 13–14
self-defense, 19
students, **10,** 32, 34, **38, 40, 43**

teacher/sensei, 26, **26**
techniques, 28, **29,** 30, **30,** 32, 34–35
throws, 28, **29,** 30
tournaments, **20, 22, 35,** 35–37, **36**
training, **8, 9,** 14, **14, 24, 26,** 28, **29,**
30, **30,** 32, 34–35
types of martial arts, 23

World Games, 36

## ABOUT THE AUTHOR

Carol Ellis has written several books for young people on topics ranging from pets and endangered animals to the martial arts of kendo and wrestling. She and her family live in the Hudson Valley in New York.